What Readers Are Saying About
30 Days to Better Love: A Guide For Men

"*30 Days To Better Love: A Guide For Men* is a must-read set of blueprints for men who genuinely love their wives." - R.E. Colclough, MA, LPC Couples Counselor

"What a fun read! Some of these I do routinely...some I do sometimes...some I should do more! All in all a great 30 day 'game plan' for bringing romance back to a marriage!" - Scott Hunter, Former QB University of Alabama/NFL

"I love this book and every marriage will be strengthened by the husband reading *30 Days to Better Love: A Guide for Men*. Drexel Gilbert's crisp writing style is easy to read and her commonsense guidelines are guaranteed to lead anyone to a more satisfying marriage."- Ron Tew, Author, *The Conversion, The Love of Wisdom*

"I really liked it, and think it will resonate with many people --men and women. It's so easy to fall into the trap of not communicating. The 30 suggestions are really good advice. They really are simple but it takes being reminded that they are important." -Diana Nichols, Creative Director

30 DAYS TO BETTER LOVE

30 DAYS TO BETTER LOVE

A Guide For Men

DREXEL GILBERT

Drexel Gilbert Enterprises, Inc.
Pensacola, Florida

First Printing

Published 2015 by

Drexel Gilbert Enterprises, Inc.

Pensacola, FL

Printed in the United States of America

Library of Congress Cataloging-in Publication Data
ISBN: 0981846483
ISBN 13: 9780981846484
Library of Congress Control Number: 2015907141
Drexel Gilbert Enterprises, Incorporated, Daphne, AL

This book is dedicated to my husband, Dr. Wesley H. Wachob, Sr.,
who brings
romance, fun,
spontaneity, kindness,
thoughtfulness, joy, and love
into each and every day of our marriage.
Thank you for your encouragement, your inspiration, and your
commitment to making
the rest of our lives... the best of our lives.

FOREWORD

Give a man a set of blueprints and he can build a spaceship that will blast off from earth and go all the way to the moon. Ask that same man to accurately "guess" the best ways to show his wife he loves her and that love will fizzle like a wet firecracker. In more than 30 years of counseling couples, I have found that love is an action verb and that men will thrive in relationships where their actions are viewed by their spouses as loving and caring. Drexel Gilbert's, *30 Days to Better Love: A Guide For Men* is a must- read set of blueprints for men who genuinely love their wives. It is concise. It is concrete. Most of all, it is powerful. It offers terrific ideas to revive and refresh a healthy and committed relationship.

-- R.E. Colclough, MA, LPC Couples Counselor. *The Centre*

If your marriage is less than fulfilling, this book is for you. If you are enjoying a great marriage, this book is for you. This book is for anyone who is married or considering getting married. When marital dissatisfaction creeps in, what began as something sacred may become stale. Author Drexel Gilbert describes the process as a "slow leak." I agree with that observation. Life circumstances, fear of vulnerability, and poor communication are three of many reasons this happens. *30 Days to Better Love: A Guide for Men* is an effective tool that may be used to repair or prevent the leak by allowing the husband the opportunity to step outside of his world and to engage his wife's world. *30 Days to Better Love: A Guide for Men* is a remarkable tool to help men make sure love is consistently and tangibly expressed day to day.

This insightful and useful book is fun, but it is not to be taken lightly. The advice should be taken to heart. It is necessary to practice habits that build a solid foundation for love and true relationship. I am excited about the impact of this book on marriages.

-Linda Hembree, MA, ALC *Christian Counseling Professionals*

ACKNOWLEDGMENTS

Special people paved the way for me to write this book and I will forever be grateful.

To Beth Robertson--- my end-of-time-friend and soul sister. You believed in me when I didn't believe in myself. Your love, encouragement, faith and prayers make me strong. You make me think... and you make me laugh! You are one of God's greatest blessings. I love you.

To Sara Neal--- my angel on Earth. Your wings lift me, guide me, carry me and wrap me up in love! Thank you!

To Gail Gray--- for sunrise walks on the beach, sunset chats in the sand, spur of the moment trips to fun places, and for being my safe place to share ideas and thoughts... thank you. I love you.

To Jeanne Tew--- thank you for sharing your exceptional editing skills.

To Jen-Beth Forehand--- thank you for your excellent cover design and for your sweet friendship.

To Quintin Howard--- my photographer, my go-to person... my friend. You're the best!

To the women who helped in the research for this book by sharing their stories, dreams, joys, disappointments and hopes--- thank you. May your relationships be blessed with romance, joy, fun and love, today and always.

INTRODUCTION

Sometimes love just stops. Dead in its tracks. Here one day, gone the next. But that's rare. Mostly, love trickles away, a drip here and a drop there. Couples begin wondering how they've gone from being madly in love, consumed with passion, and desiring to be together as much as possible to a relationship that is unromantic, routine, tired, and even lonely.

30 Days To Better Love: A Guide For Men is for the man who genuinely loves the woman in his life and wants to stop the leak that's draining their relationship of its passion. Counselors will tell you that the romantic leaks in a marriage or love relationship are a hazard of daily life. Career, children, bills, daily responsibilities and obligations (and the inevitable fatigue that goes with that list) just trickle away at the relationship... a drip here and a drop there... until the spark that started the fire way back when... has fizzled.

And you can't even pinpoint when it happened.

This book will help you begin to plug the leak. It is written in a fun and practical way. It is written with the hope that you will spend 30 days applying at least some of the suggestions. It is written with the goal of moving you toward a more playful, passionate and powerful relationship.

It's not rocket science, but it does take deliberate effort. You have to TRY. Read the book all the way through. It's a quick read. Then take one step a day, every day, for 30 days. Try them in the order they are written. Try mixing them up. The point is: TRY IT. You will be glad you did.

You say the fire's fizzled? You can rekindle it. Turn the page and be on your way to better love.

-Drexel

Day 1

GIVE HER FLOWERS
EVERY DAY
FOR 30 DAYS

I walked into her apartment and my eyes immediately fell on a vase of dried up, nasty looking flowers sitting in the middle of her dining room table.

"WHAT... is that?" I asked.

"Oh," she replied cheerily, "those are some flowers he gave me."

"Well. They're dead."

"Yes," she smiled, "and I will toss them out as soon as he brings me new ones to replace them."

Women love receiving flowers. Regardless of what they may tell you: "Oh, you don't have to give me flowers," or "It's a waste of money," or whatever it is she says... trust me.

Women love receiving flowers. Period.

Begin your 30-day journey by giving her flowers. Whether it's an expensive bouquet of red roses from the florist, or a simply wrapped bunch of daisies from the supermarket, take her a BOUQUET of flowers on Day 1.

Then every day for the next 30 days, give her at least one flower. It can be another bouquet. It can be a single stem. It can be a flower you pick from your own garden. In case of a flower-emergency, it can be a daisy you draw on a piece of paper and leave (with a sweet note) on the kitchen counter.

Oh, and when that bouquet you gave her on Day 1 dies, replace it. Remember the couple I told you about at the beginning of the page? He brought her new flowers to replace the dried-up, nasty looking ones. He still does. They are one of the happiest, healthiest, most passionate couples I know.

So pick up some petals. It'll pick up the romance. I promise.

Day 2

KISS HER
LIKE YOU MEAN IT

She received her first kiss when she was 16. He walked her to the door after their date. Her heart was racing. He leaned in and she closed her eyes. The kiss was short. It was sweet. It made her knees quiver, her heart race and her palms sweat. And, it was wonderful.

Perhaps you have a similar memory of your very first kiss... or your first kiss with the woman with whom you are spending your life. Somewhere along the line, as a relationship progresses from the early moments of its life to the years of living that life, the passionate kisses of the infant relationship morph into a peck on the lips or even the cheek. Couples begin to kiss distractedly... routinely... impersonally.

Stop. That.

FULL-ON KISS THAT WOMAN.

Kiss her when you wake up. Kiss her when you leave... when you leave the house, the room or the couch where the two of you are sitting. Kiss her when you return... from work, from the store, from taking out the trash, from the other room. Kiss her like you did when you first began dating.

Think about the famous kiss in Times Square on V-J Day. Don't know it? Google it. You'll thank me.

Kiss. Her.

Often.

Kiss. Her.

Passionately.

Kiss. Her.

Now.

Day 3

SIT BESIDE HER

You're not going to like this, but I believe the easy-chair is responsible for a lot of marital distance. A psychologist once told me that a couple's physical distance implies the level of their emotional distance. He also told me that couples who routinely sit beside each other, instead of sitting apart, are likely to be more affectionate in their relationship. I get that. It's hard to reach out and touch your sweetheart when she's sitting across the room on the sofa and you are stretched out in your easy chair.

Yeah, I know. That easy chair is comfortable. It's relaxing. It's a "man-thing."

That's okay. I get it, and I'm not suggesting you toss your chair in a garage sale. What I am suggesting is that you... for the next 30 days... spend more time sitting beside your woman on the couch as you watch television, entertain guests, read, listen to music or talk.

It will be easier, and perhaps become more customary, to spontaneously hold her hand, kiss the top of her head, rub her arm or the back of her neck as you enjoy comfortable time together.

Go the distance... from your chair to the couch.

It's easy.

I promise.

Day 4

HOLD HER HAND

I happened upon a couple recently while walking on the beach. They were standing with their backs to me, facing the water and holding hands. He gave her hand a squeeze. She looked at him and smiled, then rested her head on his shoulder. They turned back to watch the water.

Somewhere along the way, the art of hand holding gets lost. Perhaps it begins to slip when our hands become filled with grocery bags, babies, toddlers, briefcases, suitcases, or books. By the time our hands are emptied of those things, we've forgotten to fill them up again with the hand of the one we cherish above all else.

Right now, stop reading and look at your hand. I mean it.

Look at your hand.

You see that hand? That hand has the ability to earn a living, lift a child, carry a heavy box, push a grocery cart, swing a briefcase and a hammer, or hold a book.

Those are all good things.

That hand also has the ability to communicate. When you reach for her hand and lace your fingers with hers, you communicate your love and affection for her. Without saying a word, you tell her how much you enjoy being with her. You tell her you enjoy being *that close* to her. You tell her you are proud to be with her. You tell her you are happy to be connected to her.

Hold that woman's hand.

Hold her hand when you are walking. Hold her hand when you are sitting. Hold her hand at the restaurant and in the movies or sitting in church. Hold her hand when you are driving in the car. Find a stretch of beach, or woods, or playground, or back yard and...

Hold. Her. Hand.

Give it a squeeze. I bet she squeezes back. She might even turn to smile at you and rest her head on your shoulder. Wouldn't that be nice?

Day 5

GIVE HER PRESENTS

Don't panic. I'm not suggesting you break the bank by giving her a diamond or a new car every day for the next 30 days. Trust me and keep reading.

I know a man who rarely walks through the door without a present for his heartthrob. It might be a book she's been wanting to read, or a movie she's been wanting to watch, or flowers, or a sweet card he picked up at the drug store, or her favorite chicken soup when she's sick, or a box of chocolates.... just because.

I know what you're thinking.

But this is not about "things." This is not about the amount of money you spend on the present. It's about the time you spend considering what will make her smile and make her feel special. It's about the way you give it to her. With a kiss. And a hug. And a wink.

Whether it's a 99-cent card from the store, a bag of jellybeans, a carton of cookie dough ice cream because it's her favorite, or something more extravagant... when you give a woman a present you tell her many things. You tell her you were thinking about her when you were apart. You tell her she is worth the time you spent getting that present. You tell her it makes you happy to see her happy.

You tell her that SHE is the best present of all.

Day 6

TALK TO HER

"Now, just hold on," you're thinking. "We DO talk!" Really? About what?

When conducting interviews for this little book, I asked: "What do you wish the man in your life would do more of?" The most consistent answer I received was: "Talk to me."

A lot of chatter goes on in a relationship. Chatter about the kids. Chatter about the bills. Chatter about house and/or vehicle maintenance. Chatter about chores. Chatter about career.

Blah. Blah. Blah.

When was the last time you really TALKED to her? About your dreams? About her dreams? When was the last time you watched a movie together then really talked about why you did or didn't like it? When was the last time you went to lunch after church and really talked about the sermon and how it might apply to your lives? When was the last time you talked to her about your faith... what you believe and why? Or, asked her to really talk about HER faith... what she believes and why? When was the last time you drove down the road, turned off the radio and turned on the conversation? When was the last time you asked her opinion on something that is important to you... and then LISTENED to what she had to say? When was the last time you talked about how you feel about her... and why? When was the last time you really LISTENED as you encouraged her to talk to you about how she feels about you... or how she feels about anything at all?

I've heard it said that talk is cheap. That's a lie.

Talk is priceless.

Day 7

SAY "I LOVE YOU!"

"Aw, heck," you think to yourself. "She knows I love her." Maybe. Probably. So what?

You ever watch what happens after the star quarterback is blocked from throwing the game winning pass, decides to scramble, and ends up running the football 85 yards into the end zone for the... TOUCHDOWN!!!

He *knows* he did a great job! He *knows* the team, the coach, the fans, and his mama LOVE HIM. But, watch what he does. He runs to the sidelines and looks for the hugs, smiles, and fanny-slaps that are football body-language for "I love you, man..." He looks for his mama, so she can blow him a kiss and mouth, "I love you, son!"

Yeah. She probably knows you love her. But she still wants to hear you say it. And not just after she does something wonderful. She wants to hear you say it when she does something awful. She wants to hear you say it when she does something embarrassing. She wants to hear you say it when you wake up. She wants to hear it before you go to sleep. She wants to hear you say it when you walk in and out of the door going to or from here or there.

She wants to hear it for no reason at all.

I. Love. You.

Three words that will give her a reason to Read. Your. Lips.

She'll probably kiss them, too.

Day 8

DANCE WITH HER

Don't look at me like that.

Dance with her. Who cares if you have two left feet? Who cares if you step on her toes? She doesn't. She cares about being close to you. She wants you to pull her into your arms, put on pretty music and move across the floor with her: any floor; a true dance floor; your living room floor; the kitchen floor (hey, while dinner is cookin' in the oven, you can be cookin' in her arms to the tunes of Adele, or Sinatra, or Toby Keith.)

If you truly do not know how to dance... or are self-conscious to the point you just cannot bring yourself to do it... there's a remedy. Take lessons.

Don't look at me like that.

There are ballroom dance studios, classes at the YMCA or the community center, or even the church! If all else fails, there's YouTube! No, I am not kidding. Go to www. youtube.com. Search for waltz dancing for beginners... or country line dance lessons... or foxtrot lessons. I searched for 'Electric Slide' lessons and was sliding across my living room in no time flat! Learning to dance TOGETHER will make it even more special.

The point is this. Don't make excuses for why you can't do something that will add pizzazz to your relationship. Make a way for it to happen. Then, make it happen often.

Dance with her. It will be one of the smoothest moves you'll ever make.

Day 9

SIT IN THE KITCHEN WITH HER

Some of my fondest childhood memories are of being in the kitchen on the nights before Thanksgiving and Christmas. My mom would be busy with spatula and stirring spoons in hand while wearing an apron that read "Kiss the Cook." She would buzz between the stove, oven and mixing bowl with lightning speed. Instead of sitting in the living room watching television or in his office working on "important stuff," my dad would sit at the kitchen bar patiently chopping vegetables for the dressing, pecans for the chocolate pies, or potatoes for Mom's famous potato salad. They shared a lot of conversation, laughs, and love in that kitchen. They still do.

It doesn't have to be a holiday for you to put down your smart phone, close your laptop, turn off the TV and walk into the kitchen. Maybe you'll want to grab a knife and a cutting board and help her slice and dice. Maybe you'll want to pour each of you a beverage of choice then sit and chat while dinner steams and stews. Maybe you'll want to tell her how wonderful everything smells... including her. Perhaps YOU are the cook in your relationship. Super! Ask her to come sit with you while you grill and grate.

I've heard it said that the kitchen is the best room in the house. It's the room where we can share the love, laughter, warmth, nutrition and strength that builds relationships.

It's also a room that, if filled with a generous measure of love and companionship, can generate a lot of heat.

If you get my drift.

Day 10

WRITE HER LOVE NOTES

When my kids were little, I wrote little notes on scraps of paper and tucked them into their lunch boxes. I hoped they would find the notes when they needed to be reminded of how much I loved them!

My dad does the same thing for my mom. Dad's an early riser. Mom... not so much. She wakes up after him and makes her way to the coffee pot to frequently find a sticky note attached to the carafe. "I love you" it reads, or "Morning, Sunshine!"

Invest in a 99-cent stack of Post-It ™ notes. Write something tender, loving, or funny on the sticky paper then leave it in a place where she will find it during the day. Try posting a note on her bathroom mirror; by her toothbrush; on the coffee pot; on the carton of half-n-half; on her closet door; on the frame of the door where she exits each morning; in her briefcase; on the steering wheel of her car; by the case where she keeps her reading glasses; in the diaper bag.

You don't have to be Lord Byron. You CAN be, if you'd like, and that would be great! But something as simple as "I'll be thinking of you this morning," or "Can't wait to see you tonight" will help you write your way into her day and into her heart.

Want to put some romantic shock and awe back into your relationship?

Write on.

Day 11

PLAY WITH HER

You know one of the worst things about being a grown up? You don't have recess! There's no time set aside during the day to just play! We get up at o'dark-thirty, race around getting ready for the day, race off to work, race home, race through dinner, race to bed then wake up in what seems like a couple of minutes to do it all over again.

Put. On. The. Brakes.

For the next 30 days, set aside at least a few hours a week to PLAY. Have you forgotten how? That's okay. That's why I'm here.

Depending on your age and physical condition, "play" is a relative verb. But think about those days on the playground. What did you like to do? Swing? Ride the merry-go-round? Play hopscotch? Play tag? Jump rope? Play catch?

If there's a park nearby, I bet there are swings. Everyone can swing. Push her swing and see how high she can go! No park nearby? Head to the backyard and improvise a game of catch. Use oranges from the refrigerator if you have to! Challenge her to a race around the back yard. Set up milk cartons in the driveway and go "bowling."

If you need to play in a way that's less physically challenging, buy a swing for the front porch. Sit in the swing with her and have a joke-telling contest. Play the random-fact game. (Even if you've been together 25 years I bet there are some silly, random facts about you that she doesn't know.) Try to build a house of cards. If that fails, play a round of Go Fish!

Partners who know how to play with each other may just find joy in other frisky aspects of the relationship. If you know what I mean. So, call a recess and make a play date.

Spin the bottle, anyone?

Day 12

PRAY WITH HER

K eep reading. This won't kill you. Really.
Praying together is one of the most intimate things a couple can do. Prayer involves more than the physical. It involves the mind and the soul... and the heart.

You don't have to get down on your knees by the bedside or the couch. You don't even have to pray aloud. Consider holding her hand, closing your eyes and being totally silent for a couple of minutes. Pray for her. Pray for the two of you. Pray for your family. Pray for your friends. Pray for your enemies. Then open your eyes and look into hers. Tell her you love her and hug her like you hugged her when you first met. Tell her you are thankful God put her in your life.

And mean it.

It may feel awkward at first. Do it for 30 days. I bet it becomes a habit. In fact, you may decide you want to do this forever.

Forever and ever, Amen.

Day 13

MAKE A TOAST EVERY TIME YOU DRINK A GLASS OF ANYTHING!

They were in the sunset of their years. They sat facing each other in the small Italian restaurant, the candlelight easing the lines on their faces... the lines that marked out the map of their lives. The server brought the wine, poured each a glass, then slipped away. She looked at him with a twinkle in her aging eyes. He twinkled back and spoke a toast. I heard but a few words at the end: "... the woman I have always wanted in my life and by my side." Their glasses clinked. They sipped their wine. I sighed.

I thought to myself... why do we wait for "occasions" to do something special? We give flowers only on specials days. We use the good china only at holidays. We wear dress shoes only to church. We toast only if there's wine... in a restaurant... with candlelight.

Phooey!

You know what? It doesn't matter if it's coffee, tea, or tap water. Man, woman or child... if you're drinking with me then one of us is making a toast! Life is too short. Love is in short supply. Romance is scarce.

Make a toast to that woman! Look in her eyes and say something like: "Here's to the woman who lights up my life... yesterday, today and forever."

Toast her at breakfast with your coffee or orange juice. Toast her at lunch with your glass of milk. Toast her in the afternoon with your sweet tea. The more you do it, the more you will want to do it. You'll find yourself becoming more creative and I bet you'll find she becomes more responsive! She will look forward to pouring you a glass of anything, knowing that the toast is on the way. So raise your glass, raise a toast, and raise the level of romance.

Cheers!

Day 14

GET PHYSICAL

H old on, there, Romeo. That's a whole other book. One I'm not about to write! I'm talking about getting up and out and moving around.

Go for a walk. Go for a bike ride. Play tennis. Go fishing. Play golf. Play goofy-golf. Have a snowball fight. Throw a Frisbee. Skim pebbles off the lake, or seashells off the ocean. Work out at the gym. Go for a run. Plant a vegetable garden in the backyard. Buy a baseball and a couple of gloves and play catch. Find some type of physical activity that you both like to do and do it!

Do you play golf? Tennis? Softball? Do you fish? Bowl? Run 5Ks? Have you ever asked her if she'd like to do this with you? Maybe she would! If she says yes, when she tries... DO NOT LAUGH AT HER if she doesn't get it right the first time! Explain (patiently and without judgment) the technique for whatever it is you are doing. If you play this thing right... it will give you the opportunity to put your arms around her and draw her close to you while you teach her the basics of the activity.

And that may lead to....

Oh.

Wait.

That's a whole other book. One I'm not about to write!

Day 15

RUB HER FEET

Every day, women stroll into nail salons across America for a pedicure. Yes, we like our feet to look pretty. Yes, we like our pretty little toenails to be painted some pretty little color. But, hear me, Mister. We women pay good money to get a pedicure because...

WE LIKE TO HAVE OUR FEET RUBBED!

There's something wonderful about having our tired old dogs rubbed and massaged by capable hands. Oh, that feels so good. Seriously. You think I'm kidding? Walk by the pedicure row at any nail salon and take a look. I guarantee you 90% of the women will be sitting there with their eyes closed and their body so relaxed they are like a pool of liquid butter.

Now... wouldn't you like to be the one who makes her melt?

Day 16

SING TO HER

If you stop reading now... you'll be sorry. You may, in fact, be singing the blues. Alone.

Women like it when men sing to them. It doesn't matter if you sing like Sinatra or SpongeBob SquarePants. Women like it when you pull them close on the dance floor, in the kitchen, or even in the back yard, and put your mouth to their ear and sing to them. They like it when you are driving down the highway holding hands and you begin to sing along to the love song on the radio. They like it when you come up behind them as they are putting on their makeup in the bathroom on an average Tuesday... and begin to sing "You are so beautiful... to me...."

Women like it when men sing to them.

How else do you account for the billions of dollars women spend on concerts to hear men they don't even know belt out love songs to them from a faraway stage? How else do you account for the billions of dollars women spend on albums, CDs and downloads of men they don't even know singing love songs that make their hearts go pitty pat and cause their minds to drift to.... you.

Sing. To. Her.

Then get ready to make some beautiful music.

Day 17

BE A GENTLEMAN

Not long ago, I watched a couple leave their home and head for their vehicle in the driveway. He was in a suit. She was absolutely ROCKIN' a hot little black dress. He walked to his side of the car, opened the door and got in. She walked to her side of the car... and opened her own door.

Wait. Really?

Men. Walk your lady to her side of the car. Open the door for her. Wait for her to get in and get settled. Then shut the door. When you arrive at your destination, tell her you will go around and open her door for her. Then do it.

Somewhere along the way in the struggle for equality... in the battle for respect in the workplace... in the monotony of everyday life... we've forgotten that it is okay for men to be courteous to women. When you open my door for me, I do not take this as a sign that you believe I am inferior to you. I think... "Wow. Here's a man with manners, and class, and consideration for me." And that is nice.

Open the door for her. Hold her chair at the restaurant. Stand up when she gets up to go to the ladies' room. Stand up when she returns. Hold the umbrella over her head in the rain even if it means you get wet.

Be a gentleman... and that little black dress may not be the only thing she rocks.

Day 18

RUN HER A BUBBLE BATH

Whether she works inside the home, or outside the home in an office or a restaurant or a church or a day care or a school or a bank or... well, you get the point. Regardless of where a woman works... and all women work... she is ready for some relaxation at the end of the day.

Bubbles are cheap. You can buy a bottle of them for a few bucks.

Go into your bathroom. Pour a capful of bubble concoction into the tub. Run really hot water. Light a candle... or two... or five. Then turn out the lights. Invite... entice... drag... your woman to the tub. Kiss her. Tell her she is not allowed to come out of the bathroom for at least 20 minutes. Leave and close the door behind you. Take care of whatever, or whomever, needs to be taken care of.

Water is cleansing and healing. Bubbles are the bonus. Give her both and...

You are her hero.

Day 19

REPEAT YOUR WEDDING VOWS

If you are married... do you remember the day you said your vows? No. Really.

Do you REMEMBER?

It all goes by so quickly. You prepare for the big day for weeks, months, or even years. Then in twenty minutes or so... it's done. Do you really remember what you said to this woman the day you took her as your wife? Do you remember what you promised to do for her and with her? Do you remember what you promised to be to her?

Do. You. Remember?

I don't know the exact vows you spoke. Below is a sample of vows taken by millions of couples every year. Consider printing them and really reading them. Then consider repeating them with her. Some couples do this in a big-deal anniversary celebration. That's great! Some couples do it with a big Valentine's Day celebration. That's great! But it doesn't have to be on a special occasion. It can be on any Thursday. It doesn't have to be a big public deal. It can be private. On a beach. In front of a fireplace. At the base of a mountain. On a boat. In a park. In a church. In your bedroom.

Recommit yourself to her. Recommit yourself to your relationship. Recommit yourself to romance. You loved her enough to make some pretty important promises to her on that really big day.

Remember?

*Traditional wedding vows: I, (name), take you (name), to be my (wife/husband), to have and to hold from this day forward, for better, for worse, for richer, for poorer, in sickness and in health, to love and to cherish, until death us do part.

Day 20

BRUSH HER HAIR

Her hair may be one of the first things that attracted you. Whether it's short or long, thick or thin, blonde, brunette, red or gray... a woman's hair is one of the first things men notice. Or so I am told. Sure, you might like to run your fingers through it. And there's a time and place for that. This is not it.

This is the time when you walk up to her, carrying her favorite hairbrush and say, "Hey... c'mere." Sit with her back to you. Then, take that favorite hairbrush and slowly, very slowly, begin brushing her hair.

Be smart. Don't rush this. The more slowly you brush... the better.

Be tender. Tangles take time. If her hair is long, start at the bottom and work your way up. If her hair is short, it's easier to begin brushing at the top of her head and work your way down. Be gentle. The key is to turn this act of routine grooming into an intimate act of romantic love. Try it.

It will make for a really good hair day.

Day 21

TAKE HER OUTSIDE TO WATCH THE SUNSET

P oems have been written about it. Songs have been sung about it. People brave blistering heat and biting cold to witness it in places all over the globe. Why? When the colors of the sunset splash across the sky and reflect back onto the clouds... and onto your sweetheart's face... magic happens. I can't tell you why. If I could explain it... well, it wouldn't be magic.

Find out what time the sun will set each day during this 30-day journey. Make an effort to catch at least half of those sunsets with your sweetie. You may be able to watch the sunset from your front porch or your back yard. You may have to get in a car, or on a bike, and travel to a clear spot to watch ol' Sol say goodnight.

Watch it while toasting your sweetheart. Watch it while holding her hand. Watch it while you tell her how pretty she looks in the glow of the setting sun. Watch it with your arm around her. Watch it while you brush her hair.

Just watch it with her. You never know when magic will happen. Abracadabra.

*P.S. If you miss the sunset, take her outside to look at the moon. There's magic there, too.

Day 22

HUG HER

B efore you understood the power of the words "I love you," you understood the power of a touch that communicated "I love you." From infancy, we are programmed to crave the intimacy of being touched.

You want more intimacy in your love relationship? More romance? More passion? Start giving her hugs. Hug her when she walks into the room. Hug her when she starts to leave. Hug her when she's standing at her desk, or at the kitchen sink, or at the bathroom counter, or by the computer. Not every hug has to be epic. But it should be memorable...

... and it should leave her longing for the next one.

Day 23

READ TO HER

They sat on a park bench in late summer. The leaves were beginning to turn and to fall. The silence was broken only by the sound of the occasional bird flitting from branch to branch. He picked up a book she had been carrying when they stopped to rest. He began to read this book of hers... aloud. It caught her off guard. It surprised her to hear his voice reading her favorite lines. She liked it. She liked it a lot.

True story.

Alright, already. I get it. This totally takes you out of your comfort zone.

So what?

Isn't the fact that you are "uncomfortably comfortable" part of the reason you are reading this book? Aren't you trying to add intrigue and spontaneity to your relationship? Do you know how many women listen to books being read to them by total strangers... on CDs, podcasts and downloads? Well, I don't either. But I know it's a lot of them.

Read to your woman. Read something SHE likes. Don't know what that is? Take the time to figure it out. Look at the stack of books or magazines on her nightstand or on her desk or in her briefcase. If you are feeling really good about this, get a book of poetry and read it to her.

Try it. You may find she likes it.

A lot.

Day 24

WATCH A ROMANTIC
MOVIE WITH HER

"I am NOT going to watch a chick-flick," he told her as they stood outside the theater deciding which movie tickets to purchase. She sighed and said, "Okay. I'll catch it when it comes out on Netflix."

Wait. What?

Somebody hit the "pause" button. Let's think about this. You have your beautiful woman on your arm. You are about to enter a dark theater where you will sit snuggly-close to her for the next two hours and you won't give up 120 minutes of your life to make her happy by watching a "chick-flick?"

Now, that I have your attention, let's hit the "rewind" button... and rewind your priorities. You are reading this book because you want more lovey in your dovey, right? Well, watching a movie SHE likes every now and then might be just the ticket. No one says you have to like the movie. Although, you might.

Then again, maybe she doesn't want to watch some sappy old romance. Maybe she wants to watch the new action thriller car-chase, bang-bang, shoot 'em up movie. And, that's okay, too. After all... you'll be in a dark movie theater, sitting snuggly-close for about 120 minutes.

Hey, somebody hit the "play" button.

Day 25

MAKE HER LAUGH

Q: What's the difference between a guitar and a fish?
A: You can't tuna fish!

Okay... so it wasn't that funny. I still bet she'd laugh if you told it to her! Laughter is one of the most important ingredients in the relationship recipe. Laughter can help you overcome boredom, embarrassment, sadness, stress, and apathy.

Make her laugh by telling her a joke! Make her laugh by doing a funny dance while you are out by the grill. Make her laugh by grabbing her by the hand, getting down on one knee and singing (badly) a corny love song. Make her laugh by trying to juggle the oranges you bought at the store. Just make her laugh. Because, what happens next...

   ... may make you smile.

Day 26

GIVE HER COMPLIMENTS

They found each other late in life. It bothered her when she looked at the lines in her face and the graying roots of her hair. One day she looked into his eyes and said, "You know... you are getting me in the sunset of my life."

He pushed her hair back from her face, softly kissed the crinkles around her eyes and said, "Have I ever told you how much I love sunsets?"

True story.

Regardless of her age, a woman's self confidence is assaulted every day from almost every direction. TV commercials, magazine covers, news and talk shows, popular music... all send out messages that women are not young enough, pretty enough, thin enough, curvy enough, tall enough, wealthy enough, successful enough, happy enough.

Enough already.

Why not spend the next 30 days telling your woman all those things you love about her? You know... those things that attracted you to her in the first place. Tell her she has the best laugh in the world. Tell her that her eyes are a color Crayola® only wishes it could duplicate. Tell her you love her hands... her legs... her hair... her feet. Tell her she's smart. Tell her she's creative. Tell her she's artistic. Tell her she's romantic. Tell her she's compassionate. Tell her she's pretty... even when she's just awakened and has dried drool on her chin. Tell her she's sexy even when she's dripping sweat after she comes in from the gym or from working in the yard or from wrestling a cranky two year old.

Do not misinterpret this to mean that women who like compliments are NEEDY. Not true. Emotionally confident, secure, healthy, strong women don't necessarily NEED to have nice things said to, or about, them. But sometimes, they LIKE to hear those things. Who knows?

It might make her eyes crinkle.

In a good way.

Day 27

C'MON BABY, LIGHT HER FIRE

You want to put some heat back in the relationship? Strike a match. The soft glow of a candle can warm up a cold heart lickety-split.

You don't have to go to one of those foo-foo, girly-girl candle places to get your fire-power. WalMart sells candles. So does Target and just about every corner drugstore in America. If it makes you feel better, you can pick up a case of motor oil or a power tool and put it in the buggy right alongside the candles.

Place those candles on the dinner table. Place them on the tables or the mantle in the living room. Place them around the bubble bath you've drawn for her. Place them in the bedroom. Then... turn down the lights... light up the candles... and light up the night.

Oh... and if you turn off the TV and turn on soft music, you might just fan the flames....

... and set your night on fire.

Day 28

TAKE A NAP WITH HER

I can hear you saying it now: "Naps are for wimps. Real men don't need naps!"

Maybe not, Hercules. Real women don't NEED them, either. But most women like them. And they really like them when they are taken with the man in their life. That would be you.

Of course, you can't take a nap every day. You have to work, right? That's okay. At least a couple of times this month, though, slow down enough in the middle of the afternoon to ask her if she'd like to lie down with you and take a nap. Sunday afternoons are perfect for this.

Hug her so closely you can feel her heartbeat and she can feel yours. Rub her arm and talk softly with her until she falls asleep. Listen to her breathe until you fall asleep. If you can't sleep, just lie there and hold her until she awakens. You'll thank me for this one.

Oh... and forget that other excuse. You know the one. "If I take a nap, I'll never be able to get to sleep tonight."

You say that like it's a bad thing

Day 29

GO TO SLEEP TOGETHER
EACH NIGHT

"C'mon, honey. It's late. Let's go to bed," she said.

"You go ahead," he replied. "I'm going to stay up awhile and..." work on this report, check my email, finish watching this game... You fill in the blank.

It's a scene that's played out night after night in everyhousehold.com. And it is not a good thing.

There's something very sensual about climbing into bed at night with your lover, turning out the light, kissing goodnight, and falling asleep in each other's arms. I bet you did it in the beginning. I bet you thought it was pretty wonderful. I bet she did, too.

For the next 30 days, make it a point to fall asleep together. Get up in the middle of the night if you have to in order to work, or check your email, or finish watching the game you recorded. But start the night together. Think of it this way: If you've ever watched a fireworks display, you know they are a lot more spectacular at night.

Just sayin'.

Day 30

DO THE UNEXPECTED

Routine is not a bad thing. But in a relationship, routine can easily veer into boredom. It's time to shake things up! Here are some little ways you can make a big splash with your woman. Go on... try about a dozen of them. I dare you!

* Take her on a picnic. You pack the basket! Don't have her do anything but show up and smile!
* Deliver coffee, chocolate and a kiss to her at work. Don't stay. Just pop in and pop out!
* Send her an email in the middle of the day. It can be an e-love note. Or a funny joke. Or an invitation to dinner.
* Make a list of everything you love about her. Mail it to her.
* Get up 20 minutes before her alarm rings. Fix breakfast or coffee and serve it to her in bed.
* Does she have cold feet? Buy fuzzy socks and leave them on her side of the bed.
* Turn off the television and play a board game. Scrabble never goes out of style.
* Turn off the television and work a crossword puzzle together.
* Take a drive to nowhere. Or take a drive to somewhere. Play romantic music and hold her hand while you're driving. Safely stop the car. Lean over and kiss her. Then start driving again.
* Make her a cup of hot chocolate. Don't forget to toast her!
* Go outside and look at the stars with her. Hold her hand.
* Visit a museum or an art gallery with her. Hold her hand.
* Take her to a coffee shop. Sit by the window. Watch the people go by. Hold her hand.
* Ask her to go with you when you shop for clothes, or shoes, or groceries and... hold her hand.
* Remember the bubble bath? When she gets out, take her a towel you've warmed in the dryer.

* You've already dined by candlelight. Try eating breakfast by candlelight!
  Finally:
* Read aloud to her from the Song of Solomon. Seriously. This dude knew romance.

ABOUT THE AUTHOR

Drexel Gilbert knows the right questions to ask and writes in a way that connects with her audience. As a college student, Drexel found journalism to be a perfect fit and literally grew up in the TV newsroom and at the anchor desk. More than 35 years after her first broadcast, she is still asking questions—writing books, stories, and speeches that inform, entertain and help others. She has interviewed a number of famous celebrities and political figures, including the First Lady of the United States. But her favorites are conversations with everyday people who, by sharing their stories, often change lives for the better. Much of what you read in this book comes from interviews with men and women who either have or desire romance, fun, and passion in their relationships. She tackles tough issues with a light touch and practical advice that speaks to the heart of the reader.

Since her retirement from television journalism, Drexel is a sought after speaker, corporate trainer and writer in addition to being a wife, mother and friend. She encourages others to reach higher, be better, and live life with enthusiasm and optimism. Her previous publications include five children's books and a daily devotional, *Anchored: Reflections from a Reporter's Notebook*.

Drexel has two adult daughters. She and her husband, Wesley, reside on Pensacola Beach, Florida.